W9-CVA-425

THE ARTISANAL KITCHEN

VEGETABLES
THE ITALIAN WAY

Also in This Series

The Artisanal Kitchen: Perfect Pasta

The Artisanal Kitchen: Perfect Pizza at Home

THE ARTISANAL KITCHEN

VEGETABLES
THE ITALIAN WAY

SIMPLE, SEASONAL RECIPES
TO CHANGE THE WAY YOU COOK

ANDREW FEINBERG & FRANCINE STEPHENS
OF FRANNY'S RESTAURANT

WITH MELISSA CLARK

ARTISAN ■ NEW YORK

Contents

Introduction

Great ingredients demand respect, and vegetables are as deserving as any. High-quality vegetables don't necessarily need much, and the trick to cooking them well is knowing when to go all out with seasonings (garlic, chilies, lemon, olive oil) and when to hold back. Sometimes all a perfectly ripe vegetable needs is a bit of coaxing to bring out its character—maybe a gentle blanching and a minimal finish of olive oil and sea salt, or a quick sauté with a little butter and garlic. When you want to add richness, it can be as simple as grating some cheese over the dish, or adding a sprinkle of chopped nuts, which will also lend crunch. If you want to include a little something briny, toss in some capers, anchovies, or olives, or all three.

Vegetables often change over the course of their season, and it's fascinating to pay attention to the nuances. For example, when zucchini make their first appearance, they're slim and tender—all they need is a little acid, some fresh herbs, and a touch of chili, as in our Marinated Zucchini with Mint, Garlic, and Chili (page 30). As the heat of the summer wears on, those same zucchini grow plump and dense, which makes them ideal for cooking low and slow. Stewed Zucchini with Mint, Olives, and Tomatoes (page 32) is a great example of this.

Eating seasonal produce can be incredibly rewarding. When the first tart dandelion greens start showing up at the market in early spring, I'm always ready for their slightly bitter freshness to break up the starchy monotony of winter's potatoes and sunchokes. That perfectly crunchy green bean in July is everything it should be and tastes better than a green bean ever could in January, especially when paired with mild potatoes and creamy hard-cooked eggs (see page 43). And the sweet, dense squashes that come into season in October fortify us for the chill of winter.

The best place to find great seasonal produce is, of course, your local farmers' market. If you can make a visit to the market a part of your weekly routine, you'll really be able to witness the seasons unfold and change from week to week. It can be both exhilarating and heartbreaking—one week you might be able to score the first, most tender ramps, only to find they've completely disappeared two weeks later, when you've finally figured out exactly how you love to cook them. On the flip side, as much as we adore kale and carrots and parsnips, they can get monotonous by February, when they're still the only things around. But embracing the rhythm is part of the thrill.

For years, my husband, Andrew, and I did all the greenmarket shopping for our restaurant, Franny's, ourselves. On Mondays we'd go to Union Square in Manhattan; I'd sit in the car so we wouldn't get a ticket, and Andrew would blitz through, collecting everything we'd need for that night. On Tuesdays and Thursdays, we went to the Borough Hall Market in Brooklyn. On Wednesdays, we'd schlep up to Dag Hammarskjold Plaza (across from the United Nations) to see one of our main suppliers, Bill Maxwell—it was almost like a weekly pilgrimage to our veggie guru. I'll never forget one trip in particular: I'd just given birth to our daughter, Prue, and so there I was with her waiting for Andrew in the back of the car, the day after I'd left the hospital.

These days, our chefs do the shopping for the restaurants, which has freed us up to enjoy the farmers' market in a whole new way. We make a day of it. We take the kids to Grand Army Plaza in Brooklyn and wind our way through all the vendors' stalls. Our son, Marco, finds the sight of the apple-cider doughnuts irresistible, while the flowers pull Prue with an almost gravitational force. They're both totally fascinated by the big whole fish at the fish stand, and they always love visiting with the farmers. And Andrew and I can just buy what we want to feed the family for that week, without worrying about sourcing enough delicata squash to roast for an entire restaurant.

Needless to say, the farmers' market, with all its sights and sounds, provides us with a fabulous avenue to get our kids curious about vegetables. And every so often, even Andrew and I discover something new. Greenmarkets are great places to broaden your vegetable horizons, but a CSA, your town's food co-op, or even a supermarket can yield seasonal goodies. A little mindfulness is all you need to track them down.

—Francine Stephens

Slow-Cooked Leeks with a Fried Egg and Pecorino Sardo

Among the very first local springtime vegetables to appear in New York are overwintered leeks. Planted in July, the leeks sit in the ground all winter long. When the ground finally thaws in the early spring and the leeks are pulled, they have an incredible concentrated sweetness. Leeks are often in the background, but this dish lets them shine. After a quick blanching, they are roasted in the oven, where they lose most of their moisture, caramelizing and intensifying the flavor. Salty shavings of sharp sheep's-milk cheese and the runny sunny-side-up eggs make this a hearty first course. But it could also serve as a perfect vegetarian lunch, or a spectacular brunch dish. | SERVES 4

2 pounds medium leeks
 (about 5)
Kosher salt
1½ tablespoons plus
 2 teaspoons extra-virgin olive
 oil, plus more for drizzling
¾ teaspoon freshly cracked
 black pepper, plus more
 as needed

4 large eggs
Flaky sea salt, such as Maldon
Fresh lemon juice
1-ounce chunk Pecorino Sardo
 or Parmigiano-Reggiano,
 shaved, for serving

Preheat the oven to 325°F with a rack in the middle of the oven. Trim the hairy ends of the leeks and remove the dark green tops. Without cutting all the way through the root end, split the leeks lengthwise in half (see Note). Rinse each leek under lukewarm running water, fanning it apart to get to any grit between the layers.

CONTINUED

Bring a large pot of heavily salted water to a boil. Add the leeks and cook until tender but not limp, 6 to 7 minutes. Drain well and pat dry. Split the leeks completely through the root end.

Arrange the leek halves on a rimmed baking sheet in 2 rows, with the thicker bulbous ends facing outward (these will most benefit from the sides of the oven, where the heat is strongest). Drizzle the leeks with 2 teaspoons of the olive oil and season with the pepper. Roast until light golden brown, about 30 minutes.

Carefully flip the leeks and continue to cook until golden on top, about 25 minutes more. Remove from the oven and keep warm. In a large skillet, heat the remaining 1½ tablespoons olive oil over medium heat. Crack the eggs into the skillet and season with salt and pepper. Reduce the heat to medium-low and cook gently until the whites are set, about 6 minutes.

Divide the leeks among individual plates. Sprinkle lightly with sea salt, pepper, and lemon juice. Top each plate with an egg and shower with shaved cheese. Drizzle with olive oil and serve.

Note: Leaving the leeks partially attached when boiling them keeps them from falling apart. So, while you might be tempted to cut them all the way through for cleaning, don't do it.

Marinated Artichokes

When we serve this dish at Franny's, it literally flies off the menu. Someone only has to see it on a nearby table to want it for themselves. Artichokes are so extraordinary that eating them feels like a special occasion.

But there's no reason not to make them yourself at home—we do, often and for as long as the season lasts. Yes, trimming them can be a little time-consuming, but there is nothing like the sweet, umami flavor of a fresh artichoke.

This is a brighter take on the usual marinated artichokes you see on antipasti plates. Most store-bought marinated artichokes are pretty mediocre. But here the sweet thistle's flavor is rounded out with classic Italian ingredients: wine, lemon, chili, and garlic. Tossed with fresh parsley and mint, these artichokes are complex, pungent, and addictive. | **SERVES 4 TO 6**

Juice of 2 lemons

4 medium artichokes

FOR THE COOKING LIQUID

½ cup extra-virgin olive oil

6 garlic cloves, halved

5 tablespoons chopped flat-leaf parsley

½ teaspoon chili flakes

2 cups dry white wine

3 cups water

1 tablespoon plus 2 teaspoons kosher salt

FOR THE DRESSING

¼ teaspoon kosher salt

¼ teaspoon freshly cracked black pepper

¼ teaspoon finely grated lemon zest

Juice of 1 lemon

¼ cup extra-virgin olive oil, plus more for drizzling

¼ cup chopped flat-leaf parsley

2 tablespoons chopped mint

CONTINUED

To make the artichokes: Fill a large bowl with cold water and add the lemon juice. As you trim the artichokes, dip them occasionally into the lemon water to prevent browning.

Pull off and discard the outer leaves of each artichoke until you reach the pale green leaves at the center. Using a paring knife, trim away the dark green skin from the base. Slice off the very tip of the stem: you will see a pale green core in the stem, surrounded by a layer of darker green; use a paring knife to trim away as much of the dark green layer as possible; the white part of the stem is as tasty as the heart. Slice off the top third of the artichoke at the place where the dark green tops fade to pale green. Using a teaspoon (a serrated grapefruit spoon is perfect for this task), scoop out the hairy choke in the center of the artichoke, pulling out any pointed purple leaves with your fingers as well. The center of the artichoke should be completely clean. Drop the artichoke into the lemon water.

To make the cooking liquid: In a large saucepan, warm the olive oil over medium-high heat. Add the garlic and cook for 1 minute. Stir in the parsley and chili flakes and cook for 30 seconds more. Pour in the wine, bring to a boil, and cook for 1 minute. Pour in the water and add the salt. Add the artichokes (the liquid should almost but not quite cover them; if necessary, add more water). Bring to a simmer, then cover and simmer over medium-low heat until the artichokes are tender, 25 to 30 minutes. Check for tenderness by sticking a paring knife through the base of an artichoke; it should slide through easily.

Remove the artichokes from the liquid; reserve the liquid if you plan to store the artichokes before serving them. Let the artichokes (and liquid) cool completely (if you cool the artichokes in the liquid, they will continue to cook). If storing, combine the artichokes

and cooled liquid in an airtight container and refrigerate for up to 1 week.

To serve, slice the cooled artichokes lengthwise in half and place in a large bowl. Season with the salt and pepper. Add the lemon zest and juice, then add the olive oil, parsley, and mint and toss gently, so that the artichokes don't fall apart. Serve drizzled with additional olive oil.

Notes: Raw artichokes impart a bitter flavor to whatever they come in contact with, so give your cutting board a good scrub when you're finished prepping them.

To store the marinated artichokes, after tossing with the marinade, loosely pack them into a jar or other container and cover with more olive oil. Make sure the artichokes are completely submerged in the oil. They will keep for at least 1 week.

Sautéed Dandelion Greens with Anchovy, Chilies, and Butter

Sautéed dandelion greens is a classic *contorno* (side dish) in Southern Italy. Wilted bitter greens are spectacular with all sorts of big, bold meats. If you've never cooked dandelion greens before, it might seem a little odd to be sautéing something you usually think about pulling out of your lawn. But dandelions can be incredibly delicious, especially when sautéed with pungent anchovy and garlic, then mellowed with sweet, creamy butter. | **SERVES 4**

¼ cup extra-virgin olive oil

8 garlic cloves, smashed and peeled

4 anchovy fillets

¼ to ½ teaspoon chili flakes

5 tablespoons unsalted butter

2 pounds dandelion greens, trimmed

½ teaspoon kosher salt

In a large skillet, warm the olive oil over medium-high heat. Add the garlic and anchovies and cook, stirring to break up the anchovies, until the garlic is golden, 1 to 2 minutes. Add the chili flakes and cook until fragrant, about 30 seconds. Stir in the butter. Let it melt and turn a bit brown, then add the dandelion greens. Cook the greens until they are just wilted, then season them with the salt and cook until tender, 2 to 3 minutes. Serve immediately.

Note: The best dandelion greens are available in the spring. Small and tender, they are also the least bitter at this point. We prefer a dandelion variety that's dark green tipped with red, but it can be hard to find. You could substitute Swiss chard or mature (not baby) spinach.

Fava Beans and Pecorino Crostini

This is our take on *salsa maro*, which is made of crushed fava beans, mint, Pecorino, a little bit of garlic, and lemon. Use a mortar and pestle—you'll get a nice variation of texture. If you use a food processor, you'll wind up with a more uniform consistency, which isn't quite as interesting to eat. | **SERVES 4**

1 fat garlic clove, thinly sliced
¼ teaspoon kosher salt, plus
   a large pinch
1 cup peeled fava beans
   (see Note)
12 mint leaves, torn
4 teaspoons coarsely grated
   Pecorino Romano

2½ tablespoons extra-virgin
   olive oil, plus more
   for drizzling
Freshly cracked black pepper
⅛ teaspoon fresh lemon juice
Eight ½-inch-thick slices Italian
   long bread

In a mortar, combine the garlic and a pinch of salt and pound together briefly with the pestle to break up the garlic. Add the fava beans and mint and pound until the mixture has a spreadable consistency. Stir in the Pecorino Romano and olive oil. Season with the ¼ teaspoon salt, pepper to taste, and the lemon juice.

Preheat the broiler. Drizzle one side of the bread slices with olive oil. Toast, oiled side up, until golden and crisp, 1 to 2 minutes. Spread the hot toasts with the fava mixture. Drizzle with more olive oil and serve.

Note: To prepare fava beans, shell about 1 pound of them in the pod. Cook in 8 cups boiling water seasoned with ¼ cup kosher salt until tender, 1 to 2 minutes, depending on the size. Drain and immediately plunge the favas into 4 cups of ice water seasoned with 2 tablespoons salt. Drain the beans. They should now slip easily from their skins. One pound of favas yields about ½ cup peeled cooked beans.

Arugula Salad with Pecorino and Lemon

If you have superb greens, some good olive oil, and a piece of delicious cheese, a great salad doesn't need to be complicated. The arugula that emerges in the early spring, with a delicate bite, is perfect here. It's tossed with an uncomplicated fresh lemon dressing, and the nutty, creamy curls of Pecorino Rosselino play off the spicy leaves.

Pecorino Rosselino is a semi-firm Italian sheep's-milk cheese aged for about three months. If you can't find it, don't be tempted to substitute Pecorino Romano—it's much too hard and salty for this salad. Instead, look for another semi-firm sheep's-milk cheese, even if it's not from Italy. A young Manchego or the French Ossau-Iraty would serve as a good substitute. | **SERVES 4 TO 6**

5 tablespoons extra-virgin olive oil

Juice of 1 lemon, plus more if needed

½ teaspoon salt

½ teaspoon freshly cracked black pepper

10 cups arugula

4 ounces Pecorino Rosselino (see Note)**, coarsely grated**

In a small bowl, combine the olive oil, lemon juice, salt, and pepper.

Place the arugula in a large bowl and add the dressing and cheese. Toss to combine. Add more lemon juice if needed and serve immediately.

Note: Use a coarse Microplane grater (or even a vegetable peeler) to grate the cheese. This salad calls for big, coarse pieces of Pecorino.

Sugar Snap Peas with Ricotta, Mint, and Lemon

This springtime dish is crisp and sweet from the sugar snap peas, creamy from a layer of seasoned ricotta, and bright and fresh from a dressing of fragrant mint leaves, scallions, and parsley. It's almost like a very elegant crudité, and who doesn't love dipping crunchy vegetables into creamy dip? My kids certainly do, and this recipe is a great way to turn little ones on to the joys of green things. The sugar snap peas are intrinsically sweet, and they're ideal finger-food-size for little hands. | **SERVES 4**

½ cup whole-milk ricotta

¼ cup extra-virgin olive oil, plus more for drizzling

Kosher salt

¼ teaspoon freshly cracked black pepper, plus more to taste

2 cups sugar snap peas (½ pound)

2 tablespoons thinly sliced scallions

2 tablespoons coarsely chopped flat-leaf parsley

3 tablespoons coarsely chopped mint

2 tablespoons fresh lemon juice

Flaky sea salt, such as Maldon

Line a fine-mesh sieve with cheesecloth or a clean dish towel, set over a bowl, and add the ricotta. Refrigerate overnight; the ricotta will lose much of its water content and thicken.

In a small bowl, whisk the drained ricotta with 2 tablespoons of the olive oil until smooth. Whisk in salt and pepper to taste. Continue to whisk until the ricotta is fluffy and creamy. Set aside.

VEGETABLES THE ITALIAN WAY | 21

Bring a large pot of salted water to a boil. Fill a large bowl with ice water and salt it generously. Blanch the peas in the boiling water for 30 to 40 seconds, until bright green. Drain, immediately transfer to the ice water, and let stand until thoroughly chilled. Drain the peas and spread them out on a clean dish towel to dry.

In a large bowl, toss the peas with the scallions, parsley, mint, the ¼ teaspoon pepper, and the lemon juice. Stir in the remaining 2 tablespoons olive oil.

Smear 2 tablespoons of the ricotta in the center of each of four plates. Mound ½ cup of the peas on each plate. Finish with a drizzle of olive oil and a sprinkle of sea salt.

Note: To get perfectly seasoned snap peas (and other dense vegetables, for that matter), blanch them in boiling salted water, drain them, and then cool them in salted ice water. Don't overcook sugar snap peas; they should literally be in and out of a pot of boiling water—just 30 to 40 seconds—then plunged directly into an ice bath. Any longer, and you risk losing their crisp texture.

Fried Asparagus, Artichokes, and Spring Onions with Ramp Mayonnaise

As spring begins to hit its stride, some of the most wonderful vegetables start popping up at the markets. Asparagus and artichokes are both extraordinary on their own, but they are even better fried up together along with ultrasweet spring onions. Paired with an assertive tartar-sauce-like ramp mayonnaise, this lively spring mix is a fantastic riot of flavors and textures. But if you can't find all three vegetables, feel free to use two or even one. There's nothing wrong with serving a platter stacked high with crisp-fried asparagus spears or artichokes or spring onions, ready for dunking. | **SERVES 6**

FOR THE RAMP MAYONNAISE
Homemade Mayonnaise
  (page 49)
1 tablespoon finely chopped
  Pickled Ramps (recipe follows),
  with some of their pickling
  vinegar clinging to them
1 tablespoon minced chives
2 teaspoons drained brined
  capers, finely chopped
1/8 teaspoon freshly cracked
  black pepper
Fresh lemon juice (optional)
Kosher salt

FOR THE VEGETABLES
3 artichokes (about 1 1/2 pounds)
3 tablespoons extra-virgin olive oil
Kosher salt and freshly cracked
  black pepper
4 ounces asparagus, trimmed
3 ounces thin spring onions or
  scallions, trimmed

FOR THE BATTER
1/2 cup cornstarch
1/2 cup all-purpose flour
1 cup club soda, plus more
  if needed

Safflower, canola, or grapeseed
  oil for deep-frying
Kosher salt

CONTINUED

To make the ramp mayonnaise: In a bowl, stir together the mayonnaise, pickled ramps, chives, capers, and pepper. Taste and correct the seasonings, adding lemon juice and/or salt if needed. Refrigerate until needed. (The mayonnaise can be made up to 1 day ahead.)

Preheat the oven to 350°F. Trim the artichokes (see page 14) and halve them lengthwise.

Transfer the artichokes to a deep roasting pan. Sprinkle with the olive oil, 1 tablespoon water, and salt and pepper to taste. Cover the pan with foil and cook until the artichokes are tender, about 35 minutes. Let cool. Slice each artichoke half lengthwise in half. Set aside.

To make the batter: In a medium bowl, whisk together the cornstarch and flour. Whisk in the club soda. The mixture should have a consistency slightly thinner than that of pancake batter, similar to that of a crepe batter or buttermilk. Add more club soda if needed.

In a deep fryer or heavy pot, heat at least 4 inches of safflower oil to 375°F. Working in batches, dip the artichokes in the batter, then lower them gently into the oil and fry until they turn pale golden around the edges, 1 to 2 minutes; they won't get very brown. Use a slotted spoon to transfer them to a paper-towel-lined plate to drain, and sprinkle with salt while still warm. Repeat the battering and frying with the asparagus (1 to 2 minutes) and the onions (about 1 minute); drain and sprinkle with salt.

Serve the vegetables with the ramp mayonnaise for dipping.

Pickled Ramps

MAKES 2 CUPS

1 pound late-season ramps with well-developed bulbs
½ cup white wine vinegar

¼ cup moscato vinegar
(see Resources, page 91)
5 teaspoons sugar
1½ teaspoons kosher salt

Trim the hairy roots from the ramps. Separate the bulbs from the greens; reserve the greens for another use. Rinse the bulbs under warm running water and pat dry.

In a small saucepan, combine the vinegars, sugar, and salt and bring to a simmer. Stir in the ramps, reduce the heat to low, and return the liquid to a simmer.

Let stand, stirring occasionally, until cool.

Transfer the ramps and liquid to an airtight container; the pickles will keep in the refrigerator for up to 3 months.

Lettuce and Herb Salad with Moscato Vinegar

This salad is less about technique and more about shopping: you really need to use the most interesting mix of the freshest lettuces you can get your hands on.

We based this salad on *misticanza*, a mix of different types of lettuces that you find at greenmarkets all over Rome. To mimic that, assemble diverse greens with different characteristics. An ideal mix would contain something peppery, such as arugula; something soft, such as red oak lettuce; something crunchy, such as baby romaine; something spicy, such as radicchio or baby mustard greens; something bitter, such as chicory; and something delicate and fresh, such as Bibb lettuce. In addition to the greens, add plenty of fresh herbs, which you should tear rather than cut.

The lettuces get the barest drizzle of slightly sweet moscato vinegar, a little salt, black pepper, and some good olive oil. That's all this simple, perfect salad needs. | **SERVES 4**

12 cups mixed lettuces
(see the headnote)**, torn into large pieces**
16 small basil leaves
(or 8 or so big leaves torn in half)
16 mint leaves, torn

½ cup 1-inch pieces chives
Moscato vinegar (see Resources, page 91) **for drizzling**
Extra-virgin olive oil
Kosher salt and freshly cracked black pepper

In a large salad bowl, using your hands, gently toss together the lettuces and herbs. Sprinkle with a tiny bit of vinegar and drizzle with a bit of olive oil. Sprinkle with salt and pepper, toss, and taste. Add more salt, vinegar, and/or olive oil as needed. Serve immediately.

Marinated Zucchini with Mint, Garlic, and Chili

When zucchini first start showing up in the markets, they're slim, dense-fleshed little marvels that taste more like zucchini than they ever will again. They're perfectly suited for searing and a quick soak with good olive oil, vinegar, chilies, and mint.

It's a good idea to salt sliced zucchini liberally ahead of time if you can. This gives the vegetable a chance to really absorb the seasoning all the way through. Then simply sauté the slices until they're deeply golden but still crunchy. Here chopped toasted pine nuts are a surprising and delicious addition. | **SERVES 4**

4 cups 1-inch-thick rounds zucchini (2 to 3 small zucchini)	**2 tablespoons white wine vinegar**
1½ teaspoons kosher salt	**6 garlic cloves, thinly sliced**
1 tablespoon pine nuts	**¼ teaspoon chili flakes**
½ cup plus 2 tablespoons extra-virgin olive oil	**6 mint leaves, torn**
	Flaky sea salt, such as Maldon

Preheat the oven to 325°F.

Place the zucchini in a colander and toss with the kosher salt. Let stand for 20 minutes.

Meanwhile, toast the pine nuts in a small baking pan, turning once, until they are golden brown in spots and smell rich and nutty, 5 to 8 minutes. Pour the nuts onto a plate to cool, then coarsely chop.

Pat the zucchini dry with paper towels. Heat a large skillet over high heat, then add ¼ cup of the olive oil and heat for 30 seconds.

Add the zucchini and sear on both sides, without moving the slices too much, until deep golden, 7 to 10 minutes; they should still be somewhat al dente, not too soft. Transfer the zucchini to a bowl and toss with the vinegar and the remaining 6 tablespoons olive oil.

Return the skillet to medium heat, add the garlic, and cook until golden, about 1 minute. Add the chili flakes and cook for 30 seconds. Scrape the mixture into the bowl with the zucchini. Stir in the mint leaves and pine nuts.

To serve, use a slotted spoon to transfer the zucchini to plates. Drizzle with some of the marinade and sprinkle with sea salt.

Stewed Zucchini with Mint, Olives, and Tomatoes

As the summer wears on, zucchini just keep getting bigger. I may be imagining this, but I could swear I've seen zucchini grow overnight in my garden. Once the summer heat really sets in, they grow and grow and grow if they have enough space and water. So, what do you do with those big dog-days-of-summer zucchini? They're full of water, and they're blander than their early-season counterparts, but they're great on the grill, and they're fabulous slowly simmered with the big, full flavors of tomatoes and olives. Serve this dish with crusty bread, and perhaps some burrata or mozzarella. It's a perfect summer side for a family meal in your backyard or a casual gathering with friends. | **SERVES 4 TO 6**

2 pounds green or yellow zucchini, trimmed
1 tablespoon kosher salt plus a large pinch
About 7½ tablespoons extra-virgin olive oil
½ cup chopped flat-leaf parsley
1 tablespoon chopped oregano
1 tablespoon finely chopped garlic

¼ teaspoon chili flakes
1½ cups Basic Tomato Sauce (recipe follows)
3 tablespoons chopped pitted Calabrese olives
10 mint leaves, roughly torn, plus additional torn leaves for garnish

Slice the zucchini into ¾-inch-thick lengths. Transfer to a colander set over a bowl and toss with the 1 tablespoon salt. Let stand for 20 minutes.

Preheat the oven to 325°F. Pat the zucchini very dry with paper towels.

In a large Dutch oven, heat 1½ tablespoons of the olive oil over high heat. Add a third of the zucchini and cook, without moving it much, until golden, about 3 minutes per side. Transfer to a paper-towel-lined plate. Repeat with the remaining zucchini in 2 batches, using about 1½ tablespoons more oil per batch.

Reduce the heat to medium-low and add the remaining 3 tablespoons olive oil. Stir in the parsley, oregano, garlic, and chili and cook, stirring, until fragrant, about 30 seconds. Increase the heat to medium. Stir in the tomato sauce and olives. Cook the sauce until it breaks and begins to release its oil, 2 to 3 minutes.

Return the zucchini to the pot and season with the large pinch of salt. Cover the pot and bake for 1 hour.

Stir the mint leaves into the zucchini and serve topped with additional mint.

Basic Tomato Sauce

MAKES 2 CUPS

¼ cup extra-virgin olive oil
½ yellow onion, chopped
1 garlic clove, thinly sliced
½ teaspoon kosher salt, plus
   more to taste

Freshly cracked black pepper
One 28-ounce can San Marzano
   or other good-quality plum
   tomatoes

In a medium saucepan, heat the olive oil over medium-low heat. Add the onion, garlic, salt, and a few grinds of pepper and cook, covered, until the vegetables are very soft, 5 to 7 minutes.

CONTINUED

Pour in the tomatoes and their liquid, bring to a simmer, and simmer until the sauce thickens and the oil separates and rises to the surface, about 25 minutes.

Run the sauce through a food mill fitted with the large disk (or puree in a food processor). Season with additional salt and pepper as needed. The sauce will keep, in an airtight container, in the refrigerator for 1 week or in the freezer for 3 months.

OMATOES

☐ X - LARGE
☐ LARGE
☐ MEDIUM
☐ SMALL

GROWN & PACKED BY:

T. 25 LBS.
.34 Kg.

PRODUCE OF U.S.A.

NET WT. 25 LBS.
11.34 Kg.

 ☐ GROWN ON STAKES

☐ GRO

MATOES

PLUM TOMATOES

X - LARGE
LARGE
MEDIUM
SMALL

☐ BLUSH
☐ MORE COLOR
☐ RED

TOMATOES

☐ X - LARGE
☐ LARGE
☐ MEDIUM
☐ SMALL

NEW RSEY

TOMATOES

NEW JERSEY

T

WT. 25 LBS.
1.34 Kg.

PRODUCE OF U.S.A.

NET WT. 25 LBS.
11.34 Kg.

Tomato Salad with Burrata

This salad is the essence of summer, combining marinated heirloom tomatoes with a variety of different basils—opal, Thai, and regular green—and other herbs, and finishing them with dabs of milky, mild burrata cheese. It makes an ideal hot-weather lunch or light supper served with a loaf of good crusty bread. | **SERVES 4**

FOR THE MARINATED TOMATOES

2 medium heirloom tomatoes, cored and sliced into 6 wedges each

4 Yellow Rave or other small yellow heirloom tomatoes, cored and halved

1/4 teaspoon kosher salt

1/8 teaspoon freshly cracked black pepper

1 tablespoon red wine vinegar

2 tablespoons extra-virgin olive oil

FOR THE SALAD

10 Sun Gold cherry tomatoes

10 red cherry tomatoes

1 sweet white onion, such as Vidalia, cut into 1/4-inch-thick rings

1/2 cup basil leaves, torn into large pieces

1/2 cup opal basil leaves, torn into large pieces

1/2 cup Thai basil leaves, torn into large pieces

1/2 cup mint leaves, torn into large pieces

1/2 cup flat-leaf parsley leaves

1/2 teaspoon kosher salt

1/4 teaspoon freshly cracked black pepper, plus more for sprinkling

1 tablespoon red wine vinegar

1/3 cup extra-virgin olive oil

8 ounces burrata

Flaky sea salt, such as Maldon

To make the marinated tomatoes: Spread the tomatoes in an even layer on a large platter or rimmed baking sheet. Sprinkle with the salt, pepper, vinegar, and olive oil. Let the tomatoes sit for 30 minutes.

To make the salad: In a large bowl, combine the cherry tomatoes, onion rings, basil, mint, and parsley. Season with the salt, pepper, vinegar, and olive oil.

Divide the marinated tomatoes among four dinner plates. Top them with the tomato salad, dividing it evenly. With a spoon, dab the burrata over and around the salads, 5 to 6 dabs per plate. Give a good crack of black pepper over the salad and a sprinkle of sea salt over the cheese and serve.

Eggplant with Ricotta Salata, Pine Nuts, and Mint

To get the most out of this lovely dish, you need to use purple-skinned Japanese eggplants. If you can find them, the variety called Orient Express is just terrific—mild, tender, and not at all bitter—despite its politically incorrect name. These eggplants have a beautiful even shape, fewer seeds than other varieties, and a sweet, creamy texture. But you can use any fresh Japanese eggplants. Look for those that are taut, smooth-skinned, and shining, without any blemishes. As they age, the eggplants start to soften and turn brown in spots.

At Franny's, we have the luxury of being able to roast eggplant in our wood-burning oven, but a home oven cranked up high works great. The finish of mild ricotta salata pulls all the bright, spicy flavors together. | **SERVES 4**

8 Japanese eggplants (about 1¼ pounds), **ends trimmed**

2¼ teaspoons kosher salt, plus more to taste

½ cup plus 2 tablespoons extra-virgin olive oil

¼ cup pine nuts

¼ teaspoon chili flakes

Juice of 2 lemons

Freshly cracked black pepper

1 cup mint leaves, torn in half

A 1½-ounce chunk of ricotta salata for shaving

Slice each eggplant in half and score the flesh, making sure not to cut through the skin. Sprinkle the cut side of each half with ⅛ teaspoon salt. Place the eggplant in a colander set over a plate and let stand for 1 hour.

Preheat the oven to 450°F. Pat the eggplant halves dry and toss them with 4½ tablespoons of the olive oil. Arrange flesh side up on a rimmed baking sheet. Roast until golden brown and tender, 15 to 20 minutes. Cool completely.

Heat a small skillet over medium heat, then add the pine nuts to the dry skillet. Toast, tossing or stirring them, until they are golden brown in spots and smell rich and nutty, about 2 minutes. Pour the nuts onto a plate to cool.

Toss the cooled eggplant with 2½ tablespoons olive oil, the chili flakes, half the lemon juice, and pepper to taste. Divide among four serving plates.

In a small bowl, whisk together the remaining 3 tablespoons olive oil, remaining lemon juice, ¼ teaspoon salt, and pepper to taste. Whisk in the mint and pine nuts.

Using a vegetable peeler, shave 3 slices of ricotta salata over each serving. Spoon the dressing over the eggplant and serve.

Note: When you roast the eggplant, make sure to cook it all the way— you don't want al dente eggplant. Any eggplant that isn't fully cooked just isn't pleasant.

Potato Croquettes

We've experimented with many dishes from Naples, and these potato croquettes are a classic Neapolitan fritto. Andrew adapted the recipe, making it his own, by adding provolone piccante, an aged cheese with pronounced sharpness that also contributes some moisture to the croquettes. For a good part of her early life, our daughter, Prue, basically subsisted on these: they would arrive at the table piping hot, we'd cut them in half to release some of the steam, and Prue would wait expectantly for her nibbles of the creamy croquettes as Andrew and I said, "Hot-hot-hot." Kids love these unanimously, and so do adults. At the restaurant, we shower the croquettes with very finely grated Parmigiano-Reggiano. It's not necessary, but the effect is very pretty, like a snow-covered mountain. They're just a wonderfully simple yet polished little bite, and they'd make a superior snack for a cocktail party. | **MAKES ABOUT 2 DOZEN CROQUETTES; SERVES 6 TO 8**

1 pound Yukon Gold potatoes, peeled

2 tablespoons plus ¼ teaspoon kosher salt

5 tablespoons unsalted butter, melted and still hot

3 ounces provolone piccante, finely grated (about ¾ cup)

¼ teaspoon freshly cracked black pepper

3 large eggs

½ cup all-purpose flour

1½ cups dried bread crumbs, preferably homemade (see page 50)

Safflower, canola, or grapeseed oil for deep-frying

Kosher salt and freshly cracked black pepper

2 ounces Parmigiano-Reggiano, finely grated (about ½ cup)

CONTINUED

In a large pot, combine the potatoes, 8 cups water, and 2 tablespoons salt. Bring to a boil and boil until the potatoes are tender, 20 to 25 minutes. Drain.

Place the butter and provolone in a large bowl. Pass the hot potatoes through the medium plate of a food mill into the bowl. Season with the remaining ¼ teaspoon salt and the pepper. Stir in 1 of the eggs.

Spread the batter in an even layer on a rimmed baking sheet and cool completely. Cover tightly with plastic wrap and chill for at least 6 hours, and as long as overnight.

To make the croquettes: Place the flour, the remaining 2 eggs, and the bread crumbs in three separate wide shallow bowls; lightly beat the eggs. Roll the cold potato mixture into tablespoon-sized balls. Dip each ball in the flour, turning to coat, then in the eggs, and then coat evenly with bread crumbs. (At this point, the croquettes can be refrigerated on a baking sheet tightly covered with plastic wrap for up to 3 days; bring to room temperature before frying.)

In a deep fryer or heavy pot, heat at least 2 inches of oil to 360°F. Working in batches, fry the croquettes until golden and crisp, 2 to 3 minutes. Transfer to a paper-towel-lined plate to drain. Toss with salt and pepper and the Parmigiano-Reggiano while still warm.

Note: If you can't track down provolone piccante, use a combination of cheeses—about 25 percent Pecorino and 75 percent caciocavallo.

Pole Beans and Potatoes with Olives, Anchovies, and Egg

In Southern Italy, you'd probably find a similar dish served in restaurants as an antipasto. But it also makes an excellent lunch or even a light dinner at the end of a hot summer day, rounded out with some crusty bread.

No matter when you eat it, it's a lovely way to enjoy fresh, crisp green beans. Andrew adds mild soft potatoes and creamy hard-cooked eggs as a textural contrast, and the olives and anchovies provide delicious salty-savory notes.

Even better, you can prepare the potatoes ahead of time. Fish the potatoes out of the pot with a slotted spoon and reserve all the cooking water. After peeling and slicing the potatoes, instead of dressing them, simply place them in a container and pour over enough cooking water to cover. They'll store beautifully in your refrigerator overnight. | **SERVES 4**

8 ounces fingerling potatoes

4 large eggs

2 teaspoons red wine vinegar

1 teaspoon kosher salt

½ teaspoon freshly cracked black pepper, plus more to taste

6 tablespoons extra-virgin olive oil, plus more for drizzling

4 ounces green beans, trimmed

2 tablespoons thinly sliced red onion

2 tablespoons plus 2 teaspoons Nocellara olives, pitted and roughly chopped

2½ teaspoons salt-packed capers, soaked, rinsed, and drained (see Notes)

1½ teaspoons chopped oregano

2 tablespoons chopped flat-leaf parsley

Flaky sea salt, such as Maldon

4 anchovy fillets

CONTINUED

Place the eggs in a heavy 1-quart saucepan, cover with 3 cups cold water, and bring to a boil over high heat. Cover, lower the heat to a bare simmer, and cook for 8½ minutes. Remove the eggs and place in an ice bath until cold, about 10 minutes. Drain, crack, and shell the eggs.

Add the potatoes to a large pot of boiling heavily salted water and cook until tender, 20 to 25 minutes. Drain.

When the potatoes are cool enough to handle, but still warm, peel them with a paring knife. Slice crosswise into ½-inch-thick rounds. Spread the potatoes on a large platter and sprinkle with 1 teaspoon of the vinegar, ½ teaspoon of the salt, and the pepper. Drizzle with ¼ cup of the olive oil. Cover the potatoes and let them stand for at least 1 hour, and up to 6 hours, at room temperature, or refrigerate for as long as overnight.

Bring a large pot of salted water to a boil. Prepare a large bowl of salted ice water. Add the beans to the boiling water and cook for 2 minutes. Drain and transfer to the ice water to cool, then drain.

Slice the beans in half crosswise. Transfer to a bowl and toss with the red onion, olives, capers, oregano, and the remaining 1 teaspoon vinegar and 2 tablespoons olive oil. Season with the remaining ½ teaspoon salt and pepper to taste.

Sprinkle the potatoes with the parsley. Slice the eggs and scatter the slices over the potatoes. Season the egg slices with a pinch each of salt and pepper. Drizzle with olive oil. Spoon the bean mixture over the potatoes, top with the anchovies, and drizzle with olive oil.

Notes: Don't overcook the eggs for this recipe. You want an egg yolk that still has a slight degree of softness, and plenty of golden yellow color. Overcooked egg yolks can be chalky.

CONTINUED

We use capers from Pantelleria (see Resources, page 91), which are among the best available. They come packed in salt, so you need to rinse and then soak them before using.

Put them in a bowl, cover them with a lot of cold water, and let them soak for 3 to 5 hours, changing the water two or three times. In the end, they should taste seasoned but not overly salty. Once they are soaked, spread the capers on a clean cloth and let them dry out for a few hours. Then store them in a tightly covered container in the fridge for a week or two.

Fried Green Tomatoes with Anchovy Mayonnaise

These fried tomatoes are a nod to the American South. We pair the crunchy, golden rounds of juicy, firm, tart tomato with homemade anchovy mayonnaise. It puts the dish right over the top, and it also lends it a distinctly Italian flair. This is an impressive recipe to serve as a starter course at a dinner party, but you could easily serve a larger plate as a decadent summer meal, alongside a salad and a cool, bright glass of white wine. | **SERVES 4 TO 6**

FOR THE ANCHOVY
MAYONNAISE
Homemade Mayonnaise
(recipe follows)
6 anchovy fillets (see Note),
minced and mashed to
a paste
Fresh lemon juice (optional)
Kosher salt (optional)

FOR THE FRIED GREEN
TOMATOES
Safflower, canola, or grapeseed
oil for deep-frying
½ cup all-purpose flour
2 large eggs, lightly beaten
1 cup dried bread crumbs,
preferably homemade
(recipe follows)
12 ounces green tomatoes
(about 2), **sliced ¼ inch thick**
Kosher salt

To make the anchovy mayonnaise: In a bowl, whisk together the mayonnaise and anchovies. Taste and correct the seasonings, adding lemon juice or a pinch of salt if needed. Refrigerate until ready to use. (The mayonnaise can be made up to 1 day ahead.)

CONTINUED

In a deep fryer or deep skillet, heat at least 1 inch of oil to 350°F. Place the flour, eggs, and bread crumbs in three separate wide, shallow bowls. Dip each tomato slice in the flour, turning to coat, then in the eggs, and then coat evenly with bread crumbs. Fry the tomatoes in batches, until crisp, about 2 minutes. Transfer to a paper-towel-lined plate to drain and sprinkle with salt while still warm. Serve the tomatoes with the mayonnaise.

Note: Because there's so little going on with this mayonnaise, it is imperative that you use high-quality anchovies. Look for Italian anchovies packed in olive oil or salt. You're better off leaving the anchovies out entirely if you can't find a good-quality option.

Homemade Mayonnaise

MAKES ABOUT 1 CUP

1 large egg yolk, at room
   temperature
Juice of ½ lemon

¼ teaspoon kosher salt
½ cup grapeseed or canola oil
¼ cup extra-virgin olive oil

In a large bowl, whisk together the egg yolk, lemon juice, and salt. Whisking constantly, slowly drizzle in the grapeseed or canola oil in a thin, steady stream, whisking until the oil is completely incorporated and the mayonnaise begins to thicken, then repeat with the olive oil. Store in the fridge, in an airtight container, for up to 3 days.

CONTINUED

Homemade Bread Crumbs

**1 loaf or the saved ends from
several loaves of good bread,
preferably a few days old**

Preheat the oven to 300°F. Cut the bread into 1-inch-thick slices
and arrange in a single layer on a baking sheet. Bake for 20 minutes,
or until completely dried. The time will vary depending on the type
of bread and how dried out it was to begin with; after 20 minutes,
check the slices for any signs of "give," and if they yield in any way,
return to the oven for another 10 minutes. Let cool.

In a food processor or blender, pulse the bread until pulverized to
crumbs. Store in an airtight container at room temperature for up
to 3 months.

Roasted Romano Beans with Calabrese Olives

It's unusual to see a recipe for roasted Romano beans, but roasting is a terrific way to cook these lovely, brawny beans, allowing them to collapse in the oven and caramelize around the edges. This recipe works particularly well toward the end of the summer, when the beans tend to get tougher and thicker-skinned. The key is to roast them at the hottest temperature you can—high heat brings out all their best qualities, and it also opens them up to absorb the seasonings of sweet tomato paste and dark, salty olives. Serve with a whole roasted fish or simple grilled meat. | **SERVES 4**

1 ¼ pounds Romano beans

½ cup plus 2 tablespoons extra-virgin olive oil

¼ teaspoon kosher salt, plus more to taste

¼ teaspoon freshly cracked black pepper, plus more to taste

1 cup finely chopped red onion

2 tablespoons chopped garlic

3 tablespoons tomato paste

¼ teaspoon chili flakes

¼ cup chopped, pitted Nocellara or Calabrese olives

½ teaspoon red wine vinegar

3 tablespoons torn basil leaves

Preheat the oven to 500°F. Toss the beans with 2 tablespoons of the olive oil and the salt and pepper. Spread on a large rimmed baking sheet and roast until they are completely soft and limp with some dark brown spots, about 20 minutes.

While the beans are roasting, make a soffrito: In a large skillet, warm the remaining ½ cup olive oil over medium heat. Add the onion and garlic and cook until they are very soft but with very little color, about 10 minutes. Stir in the tomato paste and chili flakes, increase the heat to medium-high, and sauté for 2 to 3 minutes.

Stir the roasted beans and olives into the soffrito and cook, covered, over low heat for 10 minutes. Remove the beans from the heat and sprinkle with the red wine vinegar and torn basil. Season with salt and pepper to taste and serve.

Late-Summer Minestrone

You'll find a version of minestrone in every region of Italy. The basic blueprint involves beans of some sort, an abundance of vegetables, and, frequently, pasta; we skip the pasta in ours. With so many other elements, we feel that pasta ultimately weighs the soup down. Instead, this minestrone is about the bounty of produce.

To make the soup especially flavorful, we sauté the vegetables before adding them to the pot with the beans. Not only does this help maintain their color, it also allows the salt to penetrate and season the vegetables thoroughly, until they taste just right. If you just cook all the vegetables together in the soup pot along with the beans, the flavors of the vegetables will be diminished, since most of them will leach out into the broth. Additionally, seasoning the vegetables while sautéing helps keep them nice and firm, because the salt draws out the moisture. It may be slightly more work than your average minestrone recipe, but the results are well worth it. | **SERVES 6 TO 8**

1¼ pounds ripe tomatoes

10 tablespoons plus
   2 teaspoons extra-virgin olive
   oil, plus more for drizzling

2 medium Spanish onions,
   finely chopped (about 3 cups)

3 tablespoons chopped garlic,
   plus 1 clove

1 sage sprig

5 ounces Parmigiano-Reggiano
   rinds, scraped (see Note)

1½ pounds fresh cranberry
   beans, shelled (about 2 cups)

6 cups water

2 teaspoons kosher salt, plus
   more to taste

Freshly cracked black pepper

12 ounces fingerling potatoes,
   cut into ¼-inch-thick rounds
   (about 2 cups)

2 bunches Swiss chard

CONTINUED

**3 medium zucchini, preferably
Romanesco, cut into ½-inch
pieces** (about 3 cups)
**2 cups green beans cut into
¾-inch pieces**

**20 basil leaves, torn
Finely grated Parmigiano-
Reggiano**

Bring a large pot of water to a boil. Using a paring knife, cut a small
X in the base of each tomato. Blanch the tomatoes in the boiling
water for 30 seconds. Remove from the pot and let cool until you
can handle the tomatoes comfortably, then peel away the skin with
your fingers or a paring knife. Coarsely chop the tomatoes.

In a large Dutch oven, heat 5 tablespoons of the olive oil over
medium heat. Add the onions and chopped garlic and cook until
soft, about 10 minutes. Add the sage and chopped tomatoes and
cook for about 5 minutes.

Wrap the cheese rinds in a square of cheesecloth and knot it. Stir
the cheese rinds, cranberry beans, and water into the pot, then stir
in the salt and 5 or 6 turns of black pepper and cook until the beans
are about halfway cooked, 15 to 20 minutes.

Add the potatoes and cook until both beans and potatoes are
tender, about 20 minutes more.

Meanwhile, separate the chard leaves from the stems. Cut the
stems into ½-inch pieces (about 2 cups). Coarsely chop half the
leaves (about 4 cups; keep the remaining leaves for another use).

In a large skillet, heat 5 tablespoons olive oil over medium-high heat.
Add the chard stems and sauté for 2 minutes until tender; season
with salt. Add the zucchini and sauté for another 2 minutes; season
with salt. Add the green beans and sauté for another 2 minutes;

CONTINUED

season with salt. Finally, add the chard leaves, season with salt, and cook until the greens have just wilted.

Scoop out the sage sprig and the cheese rind sachet from the beans and discard them. Scrape the vegetable mixture into the pot. Season the soup with salt and pepper to taste.

In a mortar with a pestle, pound the garlic clove with the basil and the remaining 2 teaspoons olive oil.

Ladle the soup into bowls. Garnish each serving with a drizzle of the garlic-herb oil and a sprinkle of Parmigiano-Reggiano. Finish with a drizzle of olive oil and 1 or 2 turns of black pepper and serve.

Note: When you add cheese rinds to a soup, make sure to scrape the waxy residue off the rinds first; you don't want the wax to end up in your soup. Use a chef's knife or a paring knife (not serrated), and you'll see it come right off. Then wrap the rinds in a square of cheesecloth, knot it, and use the sachet to add rich flavor to your broth. When the soup is done, just fish the sachet out and discard it.

If you don't have rinds but want to impart a cheesy flavor, you can, of course, just use a hunk of cheese. This, however, will cost you more than rinds, so it won't exactly be *cucina povera*. But it will taste good.

Marinated Rainbow Chard

Unlike most dense, dark greens, whose stems are too reedy or coarse to eat, Swiss chard has stems that are delicious and warrant cooking. And if you can find gorgeously hued rainbow chard at the market, it would be a tragedy not to make use of all that wonderful color in the stems.

The thing to keep in mind is that the leaves and stems need to be cooked separately, because the stems take much longer to soften. So they should always be added to the pan first. Here they get sautéed in sweet, deeply flavored garlic-scented olive oil until they wilt. Then the greens are added, along with some fresh chopped garlic for pungency. This dish can be made up to 1 day ahead—and the chard is especially compelling after it's had a chance to truly marinate. | **SERVES 4**

2 bunches Swiss chard
   (1 pound)**, stems trimmed**
½ cup extra-virgin olive oil
6 garlic cloves, 4 smashed and
   peeled, 2 chopped
Kosher salt

2 tablespoons plus
   ½ teaspoon moscato vinegar
   (see Resources, page 91)
½ teaspoon chili flakes
Scant ⅛ teaspoon freshly
   cracked black pepper

Remove the stems from the chard leaves. Cut the stems in half lengthwise, then into 3-inch lengths. Keep the leaves whole.

Heat a large skillet over medium-high heat. Add ¼ cup of the olive oil and the 4 smashed garlic cloves and cook until the garlic is light golden brown, about 2 minutes. Remove and discard the garlic.

CONTINUED

Add the stems to the garlic oil and sprinkle with salt. Cook until the stems are browned in spots, 4 to 5 minutes (if the stems begin to brown too much before they are tender, add a few tablespoons of water). When the stems are almost tender, stir in the 2 tablespoons vinegar. Cook until the stems are shiny and tender, 1 to 2 minutes more. Transfer to a platter.

Return the skillet to medium-high heat, add 2 tablespoons olive oil and the 2 chopped garlic cloves, and cook for 1 minute. Add the chili flakes and cook for 30 seconds. Add the chard leaves, season with salt, and cook until wilted, 1 to 2 minutes. Transfer the greens to a plate and let cool.

Place the greens in a bowl and sprinkle with the remaining 2 tablespoons olive oil and ½ teaspoon vinegar and the pepper. Gently mix in the stems. Let marinate for at least 20 minutes before serving, or for up to 1 day. Store in the refrigerator if marinating for more than 2 hours.

Note: You can use regular chard for this recipe if you can't get rainbow chard. Beet greens will also work, though their stems are thinner, so you should cook them a little less.

Sunchokes with Almonds, Pickled Fennel, and Pecorino

There are a few vegetables that really benefit from being overwintered, and sunchokes are one of them. The shock of our Northeast cold converts the sunchoke's starches into sugar, and when the overwintered crop starts showing up in the first weeks of March, they are just marvelous.

The limited local produce during a New York winter forces us to be inventive with what is available. Pickling fennel stems is a brilliant way of brightening up a sturdy winter vegetable, and here the little bites of tangy, licoricey crunch are delicious against the nutty sunchokes, toasty almonds, and sharp cheese. | **SERVES 4**

1 pound sunchokes, scrubbed
and cut into ½-inch cubes
2 tablespoons plus 4 teaspoons
extra-virgin olive oil
¼ teaspoon kosher salt, plus
more to taste
¼ teaspoon freshly cracked
black pepper, plus more
to taste

2 tablespoons Pickled Fennel
Stem (recipe follows), with its
liquid
2 tablespoons fresh lemon juice
6 tablespoons ¼-inch chunks
Pecorino
¼ cup coarsely chopped
toasted almonds

Preheat the oven to 400°F, with a rack positioned in the middle. Toss the sunchokes with 2 tablespoons of the olive oil and season with the salt and pepper. Spread in a single layer on a rimmed baking sheet and roast until lightly browned and tender, 30 to 40 minutes.

In a medium bowl, stir together the roasted sunchokes, pickled fennel, lemon juice, and the remaining 4 teaspoons olive oil. Season with salt and pepper to taste and let sit for at least 20 minutes, and up to 4 hours, before serving.

Just before serving, add the cheese and almonds and toss to combine.

Pickled Fennel Stem

MAKES 1½ CUPS

1¼ cups white wine vinegar
3 tablespoons sugar
2 teaspoons kosher salt
1 small sprig rosemary

1 small chile de árbol
Zest of 1 small orange
2 cups thickly sliced fennel stem

In a small saucepan, combine the vinegar, 1¼ cups water, the sugar, salt, rosemary, and chile. Bring to a boil; remove from the heat and strain.

Place the orange zest and fennel in a bowl. Pour the hot brine into the bowl. Cover with plastic wrap and refrigerate for at least 24 hours before using. Refrigerate in an airtight container for up to 3 months.

Roasted Broccoli with Garlic, Chilies, and Colatura di Alici

We once went through a summer where we ate at Sripraphai, a famed Thai restaurant in Queens, at least once a week. (We still love it and have held some staff parties there.) The bright, fresh qualities of the food have always spoken to us, and for a while Andrew was obsessed with trying to translate Thai flavors into his Italian-based cooking. One of the bridges that connected the two is fish sauce: *nam pla* in Thailand, *colatura* in Italy. These are very similar pantry items—basically distilled, concentrated fish essences used to add savory notes to just about anything. Here Andrew pairs colatura with sturdy roasted broccoli, which can hold its own against the salty condiment.

We serve this cool rather than warm. Finished with lemon juice and some fiery chilies, it's a gutsy dish that quickly becomes addictive. | **SERVES 4**

2 pounds broccoli
  (about 2 large bunches)
**5 tablespoons plus 1 teaspoon
  extra-virgin olive oil**
**½ teaspoon kosher salt, plus
  more to taste**
**¼ teaspoon freshly cracked
  black pepper, plus more
  to taste**
Juice of 1 lemon

1 tablespoon colatura di alici
  (see Resources, page 91)
**1½ teaspoons finely chopped
  jarred Calabrian chilies**
  (see Resources, page 91)
**1½ teaspoons finely chopped
  garlic**
**½ red onion, sliced lengthwise
  into ⅛-inch-thick batons**

Preheat the oven to 475°F. Trim the broccoli and cut into large florets. Coarsely chop enough of the nice leaves and/or tender stems to equal about 1 cup; set aside. Toss the broccoli florets with 3 tablespoons of the olive oil and the salt and pepper. Arrange on a large rimmed baking sheet and pour ¼ cup water over the florets. Roast until the broccoli is just tender but still has some texture, 12 to 15 minutes. Let cool completely.

In a large skillet, heat 2 tablespoons olive oil over medium-high heat. Add the broccoli leaves and/or stems, sprinkle with a tablespoon or two of water to help them soften in the pan, and cook until tender, about 2 minutes. Season with a pinch each of salt and pepper, remove from the pan, and cool completely.

In a small bowl, toss together the lemon juice, colatura, chilies, and garlic.

In a large bowl, combine the broccoli leaves and/or stems, the broccoli florets, the onion, and the lemon mixture. Drizzle in the remaining teaspoon of olive oil and adjust the seasoning with pepper. You should not need salt, but if you do, add it sparingly.

Divide the broccoli evenly among four chilled bowls.

Note: Colatura can be hard to find, but you can substitute Asian fish sauce—use the best you can get. Colatura tends to be more elegant and refined, while Thai fish sauce can sometimes be a little sweet. Look for a brand of fish sauce with just fish and salt listed on the ingredients label; you don't want to see caramel color, MSG, or other additives.

Cauliflower with Pickles, Anchovies, Capers, and Olives

Served during the Christmas festivities in Naples, this dish is traditionally just boiled cauliflower paired with giardiniera pickles, olives, and anchovies. We roast the cauliflower instead to get a nice toasty flavor. Try to find Romanesco cauliflower and combine it with the common white variety—it's delicious and will add some extra color and variety. | **SERVES 4**

Two 1-pound heads cauliflower, cored and cut into bite-sized florets

½ cup plus 4 teaspoons extra-virgin olive oil

½ teaspoon kosher salt, plus more to taste

½ teaspoon black pepper, plus more to taste

1 cup drained pickles (recipe follows)**, plus about 3 tablespoons of the pickling liquid**

⅓ cup pitted Nocellara or Cerignola olives (about 12)**, torn into 2 or 3 pieces each**

2 teaspoons drained capers

8 anchovy fillets

Preheat the oven to 400°F. Toss the cauliflower florets with ½ cup of the olive oil, the salt, and the pepper. Spread on two large rimmed baking sheets. Roast, tossing occasionally, until the cauliflower is tender and golden, 25 to 30 minutes.

Transfer the cauliflower to a bowl and toss with a scant 3 tablespoons pickling liquid and salt and pepper to taste. Spread the cauliflower on a plate. Scatter the pickles over it. Sprinkle the olives and capers next. Arrange the anchovies on top. Sprinkle with more pickling liquid and drizzle with the remaining 4 teaspoons olive oil.

CONTINUED

Pickles

2 carrots, peeled and cut into
2-inch lengths

2 celery stalks

½ small fennel bulb

1 small sweet onion, such as
Vidalia, quartered

1 small red bell pepper, cored,
seeds removed

2 hot red cherry peppers, cored,
seeds removed

2 cups white wine vinegar

¼ cup sugar

2 tablespoons plus 2 teaspoons
kosher salt

Using a mandoline, slice each carrot piece lengthwise ¼ inch thick; slice the celery crosswise ¼ inch thick; slice the fennel lengthwise ¼ inch thick; and slice the onion ¼ inch thick (you should have about ¾ cup of each vegetable). Using a sharp knife, slice the bell and hot peppers into ¼-inch-wide strips. Combine all the vegetables in a large bowl.

In a small saucepan, combine the vinegar, sugar, and salt and bring to a simmer, stirring until the sugar and salt dissolve. Pour the hot liquid over the vegetables. Let cool to room temperature, then transfer to an airtight container and refrigerate for at least 48 hours. (The pickles will keep for 1 month.)

Celery, Fennel, and Pear Salad with Pecorino and Walnuts

This autumnal salad spotlights the great celery we find at the farmers' market. It's got an intense, herbal flavor that is much richer than the pale supermarket variety you usually see. We add sweet, juicy pears; anise-scented, crunchy fennel; grassy celery leaves; and toasted walnuts to sliced celery stalks. Then, as a final garnish, the salad is covered with shaved Pecorino Ginepro, an aged hard but not too salty Pecorino cheese to add a creamy complexity. If you can't find it, use Parmigiano-Reggiano in its place—it works better than the saltier Pecorino Romano. | SERVES 4

¾ cup walnuts

2 small fennel bulbs, trimmed, quartered lengthwise, cored, and sliced crosswise ¼ inch thick (1 cup)

2 to 3 celery stalks, cut on the bias into ¼-inch-thick slices (1 cup)

1 large Bosc pear, quartered, cored, and cut lengthwise into ¼-inch-thick slices (1 cup)

2 tablespoons roughly chopped celery leaves

Juice of 1 lemon

Kosher salt and freshly cracked black pepper

2 tablespoons extra-virgin olive oil, plus more for drizzling

A 2-ounce chunk of Pecorino for shaving

Preheat the oven to 350°F. Spread the walnuts out on a rimmed baking sheet. Toast until fragrant and golden, about 8 minutes. Cool, then roughly chop.

CONTINUED

In a large bowl, toss together the fennel, celery, pear, walnuts, and celery leaves. Season with the lemon juice, salt and pepper, and the olive oil.

Divide the salad among four serving plates. Use a vegetable peeler or a wide-bladed Microplane to shave the cheese over the salad. Finish with cracked pepper and a drizzle of olive oil.

Marinated Cabbage with Walnuts, Bread Crumbs, and Parmigiano-Reggiano

Cabbage has gotten a bad reputation for being one of those vegetables that is often bland and overcooked. Not here, where it is just soft enough to cut with a fork, but not at all soggy or limp. As a textural contrast, Andrew combines walnuts, bread crumbs, and Parmigiano-Reggiano with oil, almost like a pesto, and uses it to dress the cabbage. I could eat a generous portion of it as a light lunch, but I often have it at the restaurant before a bowl of pasta. While you'd never see a dish like this in Italy, all the building blocks of *cucina povera* are here. | **SERVES 4**

½ teaspoon kosher salt, plus
   more as needed
8 ounces large Savoy cabbage
   leaves (10 to 12, depending
   on size)
1 tablespoon fresh lemon juice
6 tablespoons extra-virgin
   olive oil

¼ cup walnuts
⅓ cup dried bread crumbs,
   preferably homemade (see
   page 50)
¼ cup finely grated Parmigiano-
   Reggiano
Freshly cracked black pepper

Bring a large pot of salted water to a boil. Fill a large bowl with ice water and salt it generously. Blanch the whole cabbage leaves in the boiling water for 1 minute. Remove from the pot and immediately transfer to the ice water to cool thoroughly. Drain the cabbage and pat completely dry. Transfer to a bowl and refrigerate until chilled. Toss the cabbage leaves with the lemon juice, ¼ cup of the olive oil, and ¼ teaspoon of the salt. Chill in the refrigerator for up to 1 hour.

Meanwhile, preheat the oven to 325°F, with a rack positioned in the middle. Spread the walnuts on a rimmed baking sheet and toast for 10 to 12 minutes, until golden brown and fragrant. Remove from the oven and allow to cool, then finely chop.

In a small pan, heat the remaining 2 tablespoons olive oil over medium heat. Add the bread crumbs and toast until golden brown, about 5 minutes. Season with the remaining ¼ teaspoon salt and allow to cool.

In a small bowl, mix together the bread crumbs, walnuts, and Parmigiano-Reggiano.

Place a layer of marinated cabbage leaves on a large serving plate and sprinkle with some of the crumb mixture. Repeat the layering until you have used all the ingredients. Serve.

Note: This recipe uses only the larger outer cabbage leaves, leaving you with the tender inner leaves to use for soups, slaw, or other dishes.

Roasted Fennel with Lemon and Chilies

Every element of the fennel plant, from seeds to fronds to stems to bulb, goes into this remarkable recipe: the dish is essentially a top-to-bottom love letter to fennel. It's perfect for someone who adores the vegetable, and maybe even more perfect for someone who doesn't—yet. Making the Fennel Conserva (page 74) takes some time, but it is well worth the effort.

The fennel stem confit is a great example of what you can do with vegetable trimmings. The trimmings that most of us would usually discard hold all kinds of possibilities. Here, the sliced stems are confited in loads of gorgeous olive oil until very soft. The bulbs themselves are roasted until they condense and their flavors intensify.

Danny also tracked down a very special variety of fennel seed, Lucknow, that he buys from Kalustyan's in New York City. These seeds—smaller, sweeter, and greener than the more common variety—are incredibly aromatic and delicate. If you can't find Lucknow fennel seeds, standard grocery store fennel seeds will also work fine. | SERVES 4

3 fennel bulbs (reserved from the Fennel Conserva; recipe follows)

2 teaspoons extra-virgin olive oil

½ teaspoon kosher salt

½ teaspoon fennel seeds, preferably Lucknow (see Resources, page 91)

¼ teaspoon chili flakes

¼ teaspoon freshly cracked black pepper

4 shaved rounds red onion

6 tablespoons Fennel Conserva (recipe follows)

2 teaspoons fresh lemon juice

3 tablespoons chopped fennel fronds (reserved from the Fennel Conserva; recipe follows)

Preheat the oven to 350°F. Remove the outer layers of the fennel and cleanly slice off the stems where they meet the bulb. Cut each bulb lengthwise in half, then slice each half lengthwise into thirds.

Transfer the fennel pieces to a small casserole dish and toss them with the olive oil, salt, fennel seeds, chili flakes, and black pepper. Cover the dish tightly with aluminum foil and bake until the fennel is very tender, 40 to 50 minutes.

Lower the oven temperature to 325°F. Remove the foil from the dish and continue baking, uncovered, until the fennel has reabsorbed its juices and become firmer, about 30 minutes.

Transfer the fennel to a bowl and toss with the onion, Fennel Conserva, lemon juice, and fennel fronds. Divide among individual plates and serve.

CONTINUED

Fennel Conserva

MAKES ABOUT 3 CUPS

1 head garlic, cloves separated
  and peeled
3 cups extra-virgin olive oil
3 large fennel bulbs
1 teaspoon fennel seeds
½ teaspoon chili flakes
1 teaspoon kosher salt

Freshly cracked black pepper
1 tablespoon Garlic Confit oil
  (from the garlic oil)
Finely grated zest of ½ orange
  (½ teaspoon)
1 teaspoon Strega or Pernod

To prepare the garlic, place 1 head garlic in a small skillet and pour
in just enough olive oil to cover (about 1 cup). Place the pan over
low heat and cook the garlic until tender and pale golden, 30 to
35 minutes. Let cool completely.

Transfer the garlic and oil to a jar with a tight-fitting lid and set aside.
(You can make the garlic ahead and store in the refrigerator for up
to 2 weeks.)

Cut off the fennel fronds and roughly chop ¼ cup. Reserve
3 tablespoons of the chopped fronds for the Roasted Fennel.
Remove the stems; reserve the bulbs for the Roasted Fennel. Trim
away any rough ends and very thinly slice the stems crosswise,
about ⅛ inch thick. (You should have about 2 cups sliced stems.)

In a small saucepan, warm the remaining olive oil over medium-low
heat. Add the sliced fennel stems and cook gently over low heat for
25 minutes.

Finely chop 3 of the confited garlic cloves. Stir the chopped garlic
cloves, fennel seeds, chili flakes, salt, and pepper to taste into the
saucepan and continue to simmer until the stems are meltingly
tender, with no bite remaining, 15 to 20 minutes longer.

Stir in the garlic oil, the remaining 1 tablespoon fennel fronds, the orange zest, and the Strega. Remove the pan from the heat and let stand for at least 10 minutes to infuse. The conserva will keep, in a tightly covered jar, in the refrigerator for 2 weeks.

Note: Fennel Conserva is a great addition to a piece of roasted fish. Or spoon onto grilled bread for a crostini.

Roasted Brussels Sprouts with Almonds and Pecorino

Roasting Brussels sprouts is an easy and spectacular way to cook them. After they are halved and roasted in a superhot oven, their exterior becomes wonderfully dark and crunchy, while the insides stay supple and soft. Once they cool to room temperature, we dress them with lemon juice, roughly chopped toasted almonds, and ragged chunks of tangy Pecorino. Try to find young (aged 4 to 5 months) Pecorino (see Note), or feel free to use Manchego, which is widely available. | **SERVES 4**

5 cups (about 1½ pounds) **trimmed Brussels sprouts, halved through the stem end**

6 tablespoons extra-virgin olive oil, plus more for drizzling

Kosher salt and freshly cracked black pepper

½ cup Pecorino Ginepro or Manchego, cut into ¼-inch jagged pieces (we use a Parmigiano knife)

6 tablespoons roughly chopped toasted skin-on almonds

2 tablespoons fresh lemon juice

Preheat the oven to 500°F. Toss the Brussels sprouts with ¼ cup of the olive oil. Season the sprouts with salt and pepper and spread them out in one layer on a baking sheet. Roast until browned and just tender, 20 to 25 minutes. Let cool.

Put the Brussels sprouts in a medium bowl and add the Pecorino, almonds, lemon juice, and the remaining 2 tablespoons olive oil. Season with salt and pepper and toss to combine.

Divide the Brussels sprouts among four individual plates and finish with a drizzle of olive oil.

CONTINUED

Note: When people see the word "Pecorino," they think of Pecorino Romano, but there are many different types of Pecorino—which simply means a cheese made from sheep's milk. Romano is generally used in cooked dishes; it's very salty and strong on its own, and it would overwhelm this dish.

Pumpkin Agrodolce with Almonds and Spicy Raisins

Sweet and salty, tart and spicy, this autumnal recipe has a lot going for it. Kabocha, also known as Japanese pumpkin, is the best winter squash to use here: it's dense, dry, very sweet, and a little mealy, in a good way. You want a sweet squash to oppose the vinegar—*agrodolce* literally means "sweet sour." We also add a spicy element: raisins plumped in chili-spiked vinegar; they're both fiery and juicy. A finish of toasted almonds or hazelnuts adds a crunchy texture and helps mellow all the intense flavors. This needs to sit overnight, so plan ahead. | **SERVES 4**

FOR THE SPICY RAISINS

6 tablespoons raisins

⅓ cup moscato vinegar (see Resources, page 91)

⅓ cup white wine vinegar

⅓ cup water

1½ teaspoons chili flakes

½ teaspoon crushed dried Controne chili (see Resources, page 91) **or additional chili flakes**

1 medium kabocha squash (about 3½ pounds), **peeled, halved, seeded, and cut into 8 wedges**

6 tablespoons extra-virgin olive oil, plus more if needed

4 teaspoons kosher salt

Freshly cracked black pepper

¼ cup almonds or hazelnuts

Flaky sea salt, such as Maldon

6 mint leaves, torn

To make the raisins: Place the raisins in a small bowl. In a small saucepan, combine the vinegars and water and bring to a boil. Add the chili flakes and simmer for 10 seconds. Immediately pour the liquid over the raisins and let cool to room temperature.

CONTINUED

Preheat the oven to 400°F. Toss the squash with ¼ cup of the olive oil, the salt, and pepper. Arrange the pieces on a rimmed baking sheet (or use two). Roast for 25 minutes. Check the squash; a cake tester should go all the way through the flesh with no resistance; if the squash is not tender, return the pan to the oven and check it every 5 minutes until it is.

Once the squash is tender, flip each piece and continue to roast, checking every 10 minutes, until the squash is relatively dry on the outside and somewhere between cakey and creamy throughout. It should be golden brown with a lightly crisp skin. If it seems to be drying out during this process, drizzle it with additional olive oil.

Transfer the squash to a shallow baking dish or serving platter. Drain the raisins, reserving the liquid, and scatter them evenly over the squash, then pour ⅓ cup of the liquid over all. Drizzle with the remaining 2 tablespoons olive oil. Cover and refrigerate for 24 hours.

The next day, preheat the oven to 350°F, with a rack in the middle of the oven. Spread the nuts on a rimmed baking sheet and toast until golden and fragrant, about 7 minutes. If using hazelnuts, immediately bundle them in a clean dish towel and rub together to remove their papery skins. Let the nuts cool, then coarsely chop them.

To serve, bring the squash to room temperature. Season with flaky sea salt and sprinkle with the nuts and torn mint leaves.

Beets with Pickled Hot Peppers, Walnuts, and Ricotta Salata

This is one of those dishes that transcends the sum of its parts. Sweet roasted beets are topped with salty, creamy cheese; fragrant toasted walnuts; and intensely spicy pickled peppers. Every bite is different—some spicier, some sweeter, some creamier. Harmonious and utterly compelling, this is one of our most popular winter offerings. | **SERVES 6**

6 medium beets (1 ¾ pounds)
¾ cup extra-virgin olive oil
5 teaspoons kosher salt, plus more for sprinkling
¼ cup plus ½ teaspoon red wine vinegar

Freshly cracked black pepper
1 ½ cups walnuts
1 tablespoon Pickled Hot Peppers (recipe follows)
2 cups shaved ricotta salata (8 ounces)

Preheat the oven to 375°F. Place the beets in a roasting pan with sides that are higher than the beets. Drizzle with 2 tablespoons of the olive oil, sprinkle with 4 teaspoons of the salt, and toss to combine. Sprinkle 6 tablespoons water and 2 tablespoons of the vinegar over the beets. Cover the pan with aluminum foil and bake until the beets are tender, 1 to 1 ½ hours. Remove from the oven and let cool; reduce the oven temperature to 325°F.

Peel the beets and slice into ½-inch-thick rounds. Arrange in a single layer on a rimmed baking sheet. Sprinkle with 2 tablespoons olive oil, 2 teaspoons vinegar, ½ teaspoon salt, and pepper to taste. Cover the beets with plastic wrap and refrigerate for at least 2 hours, and up to 3 days. (If marinating for less than 3 hours, you can let them stand at room temperature.)

CONTINUED

Meanwhile, spread the walnuts on a rimmed baking sheet. Toast until golden and fragrant, 10 to 12 minutes. Cool, and break into pieces with your hands.

Gently toss the beets with 6 tablespoons olive oil, the pickled peppers, and the remaining 1½ tablespoons vinegar and ½ teaspoon salt. Toss in the walnuts.

Spread the beet mixture on a large plate. Top with the ricotta, drizzle with the remaining 2 tablespoons olive oil, and sprinkle with salt.

Pickled Hot Peppers

MAKES ABOUT 1 CUP

8 ounces mixed hot peppers, such as Hungarian hot wax, Anaheim, cayenne, jalapeño, serrano, cherry, and/or banana peppers, cored and seeded
1 cup white wine vinegar

½ cup moscato vinegar (see Resources, page 91)
¼ cup sugar
1 tablespoon kosher salt
1 ounce small hot peppers, such as habanero, Scotch bonnet, Granada, ghost, Brazilian bird, or Thai bird, seeded

In a medium saucepan, combine the peppers, vinegars, sugar, and salt and bring to a simmer.

Place the small hot peppers in a bowl. Pour the hot mixture over the peppers. Cool to room temperature, then transfer to an airtight container and refrigerate for 1 week.

Remove the peppers and finely chop, then return them to their pickling brine. The peppers will keep, tightly covered, in the refrigerator for 6 months or longer.

Chickpea and Kale Soup

As far as we know, there's no classic Italian soup made with chickpeas and kale. This was born out of our love for the combination of Tuscan kale and chickpeas, which work beautifully together. Andrew came up with the recipe one day when he noticed that the broth left from cooking chickpeas was so delicious it was practically begging to be made into soup. So he did just that, adding fresh kale to the pot and letting it simmer until soft and silky. With its bright, deeply green color, this soup is as beautiful as it is delicious. | **SERVES 8 TO 10**

2 cups dried chickpeas

1 carrot, peeled and cut into large chunks

1 celery stalk, cut into large chunks

1 onion, halved

11 garlic cloves

5 strips lemon peel

1 rosemary sprig

1 tablespoon kosher salt, or more to taste

3½ quarts water

1½ cups plus 2 tablespoons extra-virgin olive oil, plus more for drizzling

¼ teaspoon chili flakes

2 bunches Tuscan kale

Freshly cracked black pepper

Lemon wedges

Finely grated Parmigiano-Reggiano

Place the chickpeas in a large bowl and cover with plenty of water. Let soak for 8 hours or overnight; drain.

Wrap the carrot, celery, onion, 3 garlic cloves, the lemon peel, and rosemary in a large square of cheesecloth and secure with kitchen twine or a tight knot.

CONTINUED

In a large pot, combine the sachet of vegetables, the chickpeas, salt, water, and 1 cup of the olive oil. Bring to a boil over high heat, then reduce the heat to medium-low and simmer until the chickpeas are tender, about 1 hour.

Meanwhile, finely chop the remaining 8 garlic cloves. In a small skillet, heat 3 tablespoons olive oil over medium heat. Add the garlic and chili flakes and cook until the garlic is fragrant but not golden, about 1 minute. Remove from the heat.

Remove the center ribs from the kale and coarsely chop the leaves (you should have about 16 cups). In a large skillet, heat the remaining 7 tablespoons olive oil over medium-high heat. Add the kale in batches and cook, tossing occasionally, until tender, about 3 minutes. Remove from the heat.

When the chickpeas are cooked, combine the kale, garlic oil, 2 cups of the chickpeas, and 1 cup of the cooking liquid in a food processor and puree until smooth. Return the puree to the pot and cook over medium-high heat until hot. Season with salt and pepper to taste.

Ladle the soup into bowls. Finish with a squeeze of lemon, some grated Parmigiano-Reggiano, and a drizzle of olive oil.

Citrus Salad with Pistachios, Olives, and Chilies

If you like to keep a variety of fragrant citrus fruits on hand in winter, this is an ideal way to turn them into a juicy and satisfying last-minute lunch. Feel free to vary the types of citrus, letting the recipe evolve throughout their winter season: satsumas, Minneolas, tangerines, Cara Caras, blood oranges, and grapefruit can all make an appearance as they show up in your local market. The mix of colorful citrus, pistachios, briny olives, and pickled hot peppers is a surprisingly bright and piquant combination—especially in the winter, when flavors tend to be more muted and our tastes run toward richer food. | **SERVES 4**

2 small pink grapefruits
2 blood oranges
2 navel or Cara Cara oranges
2 tangerines
Scant ¼ teaspoon flaky sea salt, such as Maldon, plus a pinch
Pinch of freshly cracked black pepper
2 tablespoons red wine vinegar
2 tablespoons extra-virgin olive oil, plus more for drizzling

¼ cup Castelvetrano or other mild, meaty green olives, pitted and sliced
1½ tablespoons minced red onion
2 tablespoons chopped fresh flat-leaf parsley
¾ teaspoon Pickled Hot Peppers (page 84)
3 tablespoons plus 1 teaspoon toasted pistachios

Slice the ends from the grapefruit and stand each one upright on a flat surface. Use a sharp knife to cut away the rind and white pith in

strips from top to bottom, following the contour of the fruit. Cut the fruit into ¼-inch-thick wheels. Pick out and discard the seeds.

Peel the oranges. Remove any remaining white pith and slice the oranges into ¼-inch-thick wheels. Pick out and discard the seeds. Peel the tangerines, remove any remaining white pith, and separate the tangerines into segments. Remove any seeds with a paring knife.

Arrange the citrus on a large plate, mixing the colors and shapes. Sprinkle with the pinch of sea salt (this will bring out and intensify the flavor of the fruit without making it salty). Season with the pepper.

In a small bowl, stir together the vinegar, olive oil, olives, red onion, parsley, hot peppers, pistachios, and the remaining scant ¼ teaspoon salt.

Spoon the dressing over the citrus. Drizzle generously with olive oil and serve.

Resources

Italian Pantry Items

Salt-packed capers from
Pantelleria, moscato vinegar,
Tutto Calabria Calabrian chilies
packed in oil, colatura di alici,
high-quality anchovies, excellent
olive oils, San Marzano tomatoes

bklynlarder.com
buonitalia.com
gustiamo.com

Note: For a cheater's moscato
vinegar substitute, whisk together
½ cup apple cider vinegar,
2½ teaspoons honey, and
¼ teaspoon balsamic vinegar.

Dried Herbs and Spices

Lucknow fennel seeds, Controne
chili, and more

bklynlarder.com
kalustyans.com
madecasse.com
manicaretti.com
thespicehouse.com

Spirits and Liqueurs

For grappas, amari, and liqueurs

wine-searcher.com

Index

Conversion Charts

Here are rounded-off equivalents between the metric system and the traditional systems that are used in the United States to measure weight and volume.

FRACTIONS / DECIMALS

FRACTIONS	DECIMALS
⅛	.125
¼	.25
⅓	.33
⅜	.375
½	.5
⅝	.625
⅔	.67
¾	.75
⅞	.875

WEIGHTS

US/UK	METRIC
¼ oz	7 g
½ oz	15 g
1 oz	30 g
2 oz	55 g
3 oz	85 g
4 oz	110 g
5 oz	140 g
6 oz	170 g
7 oz	200 g
8 oz (½ lb)	225 g
9 oz	250 g
10 oz	280 g
11 oz	310 g
12 oz	340 g
13 oz	370 g
14 oz	400 g
15 oz	425 g
16 oz (1 lb)	455 g

VOLUME

AMERICAN	IMPERIAL	METRIC
¼ tsp		1.25 ml
½ tsp		2.5 ml
1 tsp		5 ml
½ Tbsp (1½ tsp)		7.5 ml
1 Tbsp (3 tsp)		15 ml
¼ cup (4 Tbsp)	2 fl oz	60 ml
⅓ cup (5 Tbsp)	2½ fl oz	75 ml
½ cup (8 Tbsp)	4 fl oz	125 ml
⅔ cup (10 Tbsp)	5 fl oz	150 ml
¾ cup (12 Tbsp)	6 fl oz	175 ml
1 cup (16 Tbsp)	8 fl oz	250 ml
1¼ cups	10 fl oz	300 ml
1½ cups	12 fl oz	350 ml
2 cups (1 pint)	16 fl oz	500 ml
2½ cups	20 fl oz (1 pint)	625 ml
5 cups	40 fl oz (1 qt)	1.25 l

OVEN TEMPERATURES

	°F	°C	GAS MARK
very cool	250–275	130–140	½–1
cool	300	148	2
warm	325	163	3
moderate	350	177	4
moderately hot	375–400	190–204	5–6
hot	425	218	7
very hot	450–475	232–245	8–9

°C/F TO °F/C CONVERSION CHART

°C/F	°C	°F	°C/F	°C	°F	°C/F	°C	°F	°C/F	°C	°F
90	32	194	220	104	428	350	177	662	480	249	896
100	38	212	230	110	446	360	182	680	490	254	914
110	43	230	240	116	464	370	188	698	500	260	932
120	49	248	250	121	482	380	193	716	510	266	950
130	54	266	260	127	500	390	199	734	520	271	968
140	60	284	270	132	518	400	204	752	530	277	986
150	66	302	280	138	536	410	210	770	540	282	1,004
160	71	320	290	143	554	420	216	788	550	288	1,022
170	77	338	300	149	572	430	221	806			
180	82	356	310	154	590	440	227	824			
190	88	374	320	160	608	450	232	842			
200	93	392	330	166	626	460	238	860			
210	99	410	340	171	644	470	243	878			

Example: If your temperature is 90°F, your conversion is 32°C; if your temperature is 90°C, your conversion is 194°F.

Library of Congress Cataloging-in-Publication Data

Names: Feinberg, Andrew, 1974– author. | Stephens, Francine, author. | Clark, Melissa, author.
Title: The artisanal kitchen : vegetables the Italian way / Andrew Feinberg,
    Francine Stephens, Melissa Clark.
Description: New York : Artisan, a division of Workman
    Publishing Company, Inc. [2017]
Identifiers: LCCN 2016034063 | ISBN 9781579657642
    (hardback, paper over board)
Subjects: LCSH: Cooking (Vegetables)–Italy. | Seasonal cooking–
    Italy. | Cooking, Italian. | LCGFT: Cookbooks.
Classification: LCC TX801 .F45 2017 | DDC 641.6/50945–dc23
LC record available at https://lccn.loc.gov/2016034063

Artisan books are available at special discounts when purchased in bulk for premiums and sales promotions as well as for fund-raising or educational use. Special editions or book excerpts also can be created to specification. For details, contact the Special Sales Director at the address below, or send an e-mail to specialmarkets@workman.com.

Published by Artisan
A division of Workman Publishing Co., Inc.
225 Varick Street
New York, NY 10014-4381
artisanbooks.com

Artisan is a registered trademark of Workman Publishing Co., Inc.

Portions of this book have been adapted from material that appears in *Franny's: Simple Seasonal Italian* (Artisan, 2013).

Published simultaneously in Canada by Thomas Allen & Son, Limited

Printed in China
First printing, May 2017

10 9 8 7 6 5 4 3 2 1